Who Works Here?

POLICE

Police Station

by Lola M. Schaefer

Heinemann Library
Chicago, Illinois

Published by Heinemann Library,
an imprint of Reed Educational & Professional Publishing,
100 N. LaSalle, Suite 1010
Chicago, IL 60602
Customer Service 888-454-2279

Printed in Hong Kong
Designed by Made in Chicago Design Associates

04 03 02 01 00
10 9 8 7 6 5 4 3 2 1

Library of Congress Cataloging-in-Publication Data
Schaefer, Lola M., 1950
    Police station / Lola Schaefer.
      p. cm. – (Who works here?)
    Includes bibliographical references and index.
    Summary: Introduces the officers who work in a police station.
including the Chief of Police, patrol officers, canine officers,
detectives, the crime scene technician, and the laboratory
supervisor.
    ISBN 1-57572-520-7 (library binding)
    1. Police Juvenile literature. 2. Police- -United States Juvenile
literature [1. Police. 2. Occupations.] I. Title. II. Series.
HV7922.S33 2000
363.2'0973—dc21
                                      99-40768
                                           CIP

Acknowledgments
All photographs by Phil Martin.

Special thanks to Officer Dale Davis and the rest of the staff at Fort Wayne Police Headquarters
in Fort Wayne, Indiana, and to workers everywhere who take pride in what they do.

Some words are shown in bold, **like this.**
You can find out what they mean by looking in the glossary.

Contents

What Is a Police Station?

A police station is a building where police officers work. It is open 24 hours a day. **Citizens** can walk into the station with a police problem and receive help. They can telephone 911 for emergency **services,** or they can stop and ask a patrol officer for help.

Some officers patrol the streets, parks, and neighborhoods in cars or on bikes. Other officers **record** information at the police station. Many officers work together to solve crimes. Police officers work to keep their **communities** safe.

Police officers like to meet the people in their community. They are there to help you.

This police station is in Fort Wayne, Indiana. This map shows where all the people in this book are working. Many police stations in the United States have the same departments.

Sixth Floor
- Narcotics division

Fifth Floor
- Administration
- Chief of Police
- Internal Affairs
- Public Affairs
- Planning and Research
- Computer Specialist

Fourth Floor
- Crime Scene Unit
- Crime Lab
- Property Room

Third Floor
- Detectives
- Juvenile Aid
- Crime Analysis Unit

Second Floor
- Operations Division
- Traffic Unit

First Floor
- Front Desk
- Records Bureau
- Victim Assistance
- Crime Prevention Unit

Basement
- Dispatcher
- Bicycle Maintenance and Storage

Chief of Police

Dan is the Chief of Police. He can locate all the patrol cars in the city with his computer.

The Chief of Police is responsible for everything that happens in the police department. Usually, a **mayor** of the city chooses the Chief of Police. Each week, the chief talks with officers about ways to stop crime.

A police officer usually needs at least fifteen years on the **force** before he or she can become Chief of Police. Dan, like many Chiefs of Police, enjoys working with fellow officers. Together they help make plans to prevent crime in the **community**.

Here, Dan and the Assistant Chief talk about car thefts in the city.

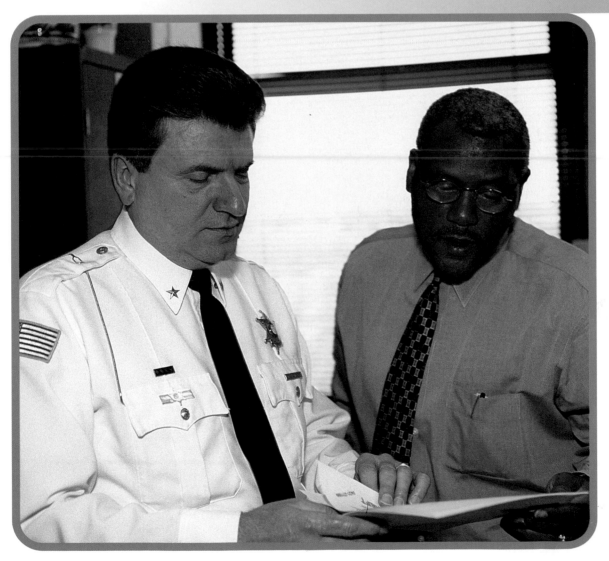

Dispatcher

Angie is a dispatcher. Here she receives a call
from a citizen reporting an accident.

A dispatcher receives calls from **citizens** who dial 911.
When a citizen needs a police officer, the citizen gives
the dispatcher his or her name and address. Using a radio,
the dispatcher quickly contacts the police and gives them
the information.

Like many dispatchers, Angie trained six months on the job with another dispatcher. Dispatchers must learn to use special communications equipment. They study the land features and buildings of the **communities** in which they live, as well as all the street names. They learn how to keep callers calm while asking the right questions.

Angie calls the water department about a broken water pipe.

Patrol Officer

A patrol officer drives or walks through neighborhoods. If someone breaks the law, the patrol officer stops and makes an arrest. Patrol officers also look for **reckless** drivers. If the dispatcher calls the patrol officer on the radio, the patrol officer **responds** right away.

This patrol officer is typing a report on the computer in his patrol car.

This is Patrol Officer Kenneth. He often speaks with children so they learn to trust patrol officers.

Special equipment in the police cars helps the officers do their job. Video recorders take moving pictures out their front windows. Patrol officers can **record** traffic and license numbers. They can speak with **witnesses** to accidents and crimes.

Bike Patrol Officer

This is Patrol Officer Dale. He is a bike patrol officer. He begins his patrol at the police station.

Some officers patrol city streets on bicycles. Their uniforms are shorts and a shirt with the word *POLICE* on the back. Bike patrol officers carry radios on lightweight belts. To protect their heads, bike patrol officers always wear helmets.

Police officers must take a three-day training course before joining the bike patrol. They must have the strength to ride long distances. They learn how to ride up and down stairs and how to use the bicycle to control a **suspect**.

Dale checks the air in his tires for speed and safety.

Canine Officer

A **canine** officer works with dogs that are trained to do police work. The police dog has a sense of smell six hundred times greater than a human. This keen sense helps police dogs track **suspects** and find **evidence** for their canine officers.

When Canine Officer Robert calls his dog Rico, the dog jumps out the window to join him.

292

FORT WAYNE
POLICE
INDIANA

14

Rico listens and obeys as Officer Robert commands the police dog to sit.

Canine officers and their dogs train together for several weeks to become a patrol team. Police dogs must learn to obey the officer's commands. The team continues to practice police drills each week. As a reward for a job well done, the officer lets the dog play with a favorite toy.

Emergency Services Team Commander

Officer Kevin is the commander of an emergency services team. He uses a computer to communicate with the police station.

The emergency **services** team **responds** to dangerous police situations. The team's leader is called the commander. The commander uses a special police vehicle as a **command post.** When called into action, the commander must first **organize** his team at the scene. Then, the team removes other people from the area.

Kevin, like all officers, went to the Police Academy for twenty weeks. To join the emergency services team, officers must get special training. Emergency services team members continue training at local and state meetings. Everything they learn helps them protect the **public**.

A commander needs to prepare quickly to take charge of his team.

17

Using Emergency Services Gear

A commander of an emergency **services** team stores the equipment in the back of a truck. The commander travels with a rescue rope and protective uniform. The commander also brings tools that could be used to break into a building.

Officer Kevin gives instructions to his team using a radio attached to his uniform.

The commander carries more gear in the pockets on his uniform.

High-risk police situations are dangerous. The commander's protective uniform helps keep him safe. He wears a bullet **resistant** vest, safety glasses, gloves, and boots. He wears knee and elbow pads for crawling on hard surfaces. His helmet protects his head.

Detective

David is a detective. He often checks out clues by talking to people on the telephone.

A detective **investigates** crimes against people. When the detective arrives at the crime scene, he or she talks to the officer in charge and tries to get a description of the **suspect**. The detective talks with **witnesses** and takes notes.

Detectives usually wear street clothes when working. A detective works with other officers while working on a **case.** The detective collects information, visits the crime lab, and studies **evidence.** Most detectives enjoy problem-solving to find and arrest suspects.

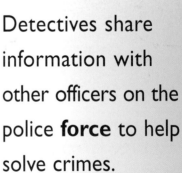

Detectives share information with other officers on the police **force** to help solve crimes.

Crime Scene Technician

Chris, a crime scene technician, labels evidence in the storage room.

A crime scene technician is called when a death is not from natural causes. The technician meets with the **responding** officer and the detective. The crime scene technician uses police tape to keep people away from the crime scene. This makes it easier to search for **evidence.**

At the crime scene, the technician makes a
video recording of the inside and outside of
the area. The technician collects all evidence
and fingerprints. Back at the police station,
the technician files a report of the **case.**

Chris then boxes all the evidence for
a case and locks it up.

Laboratory Supervisor

This is David. He is a laboratory supervisor. Here he studies a set of ink fingerprints.

A laboratory supervisor helps solve crimes by removing **latent** fingerprints from **evidence** and comparing them with ink fingerprints. A laboratory supervisor also matches palm prints, footprints, and tire prints. Laboratory supervisors often appear in **court** to present the results of their work.

To become a laboratory supervisor, a police officer needs extra training. Most go to the **FBI** Academy for three weeks. Then an officer must get more training to become a supervisor. Each year, laboratory supervisors continue to learn more. Laboratory supervisors must learn to use the newest equipment and information to solve crimes.

David uses a computer to enlarge and match fingerprints.

Using Laboratory Equipment

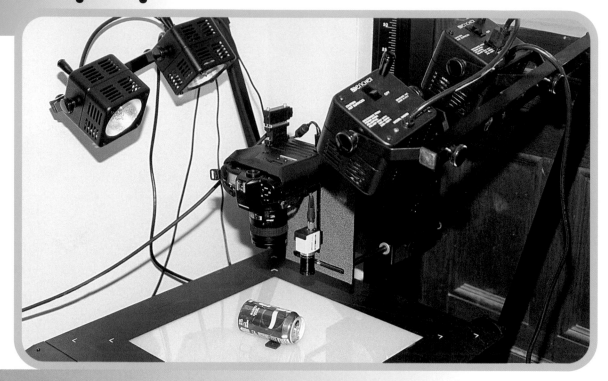

There are fingerprints on this can. David uses the camera to take pictures of the can and to send them to the computer.

All crime laboratories have cameras to **record evidence.** A special camera takes pictures of **latent** fingerprints on objects. The camera sends the picture to a computer. The computer makes the image larger and clearer. Then David will compare the fingerprint from the can with an ink fingerprint.

A special machine called a vacuum chamber helps non-visible fingerprints become visible. Evidence is placed in the chamber and the chamber is closed. Using special chemicals and heat, the chamber makes fingerprints visible. Then the fingerprints can be photographed.

Here, David places evidence into the chamber.

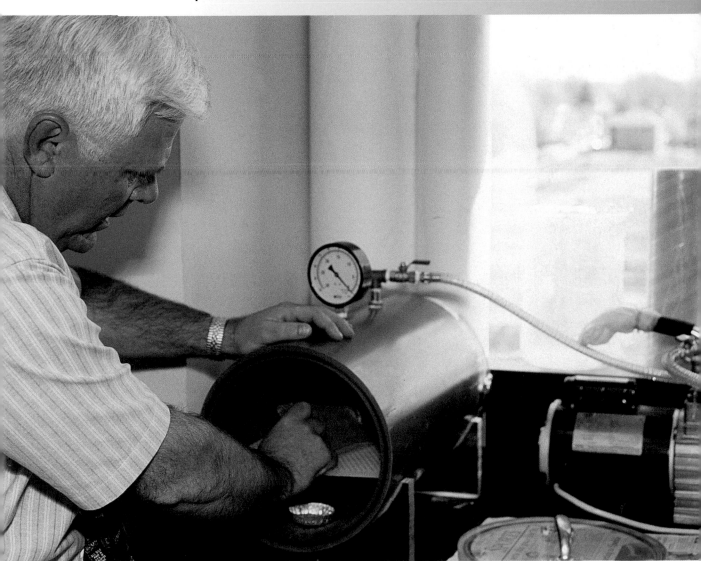

Safety Officer

A safety officer teaches **pedestrian** safety to young school children. Safety officers often present programs in a classroom. The safety officer teaches children how to cross streets at corners and how to obey traffic signals. The children practice with the officer.

This is Safety Village Officer Audrey. She teaches children how to cross streets safely.

Safety Village Officer Audrey reviews the safety rules before the children enter the safety village.

Some **communities** have built "safety villages." Local businesses pitched in to help build a model of a city. Buildings and streets are sized for the children. Using a safety village, safety officers can give special programs. Children practice pedestrian safety on the model village streets.

Glossary

canine another word for dog

case another word for a crime and the investigation of it

citizen person who lives in a town, city, or country

command post headquarters during an emergency or other event

community area where people live, work, and shop

court place where a group of people decide if someone has broken the law and what punishment should be given

evidence information, facts, and objects that are used to solve a crime

FBI (Federal Bureau of Investigation) part of the U. S. government that solves serious crimes and protects the government

force another word for police department

investigate to find out as much as possible about something

latent present but not very strong or visible

mayor leader of a town or city

narcotics another word for drugs

organize to plan and put things and people in order

pedestrian someone who travels by walking

public people of a country, state, or town

reckless careless about safety

record to write down or save information so it can be looked at again

resistant can stop or slow the movement of another object

respond to react to a call, warning, or announcement

service to give help

suspect someone thought to be guilty of a crime

witness person who has seen or heard something

More Books to Read

Cooper, Jason. *Police Stations.* Vero Beach, Fla.: Rourke Publishers, 1992.

Greene, Carol. *At the Police Station.* Plymouth, Minn.: Child's World, 1997.

Kallen, Stuart. *The Police Station.* Minneapolis, Minn.: ABDO & Daughters, 1997.

Winkleman, Katherine K. *Police Patrol.* New York: Walker & Co., 1996.

Index